APPARITIONS OF

CHRIS SPALT

All words, artwork, photography, design and layout by **Chris Spalton**

Cover art by Smalls (@Smallstattooing) Fonts by Jon Gibson (@studio.buchanan)
Printed by Rich Hardiman at www.comicprintinguk.com

THANKS FOR INSPIRATION AND PRIOR RESEARCH:

Mike Burgess
Peter Tolhurst
Nick Stone
Siofra Connor/Stacia Briggs

www.hiddenea.com
Author of This Hollow Land
www.Invisibleworks.co.uk
Weird Norfolk/Weird Suffolk

SPECIAL THANKS TO SARAH PURSEY FOR TOLERATING MY INDULGENCES

ISBN NUMBER: 9781999676728

TWITTER: @CHRISSPALTON | INSTAGRAM: @SPALTON | EMAIL: CSPALTON@GMAIL.COM

GROWING UP IN A REMOTE RURAL VILLAGE, YOU'RE SURROUNDED BY STORIES AND STRANGENESS.

They're everywhere: snippets overheard in the village shop, spooky tales passed down by relations and relayed to friends, rumours and murmurs of odd folk, strange barns, clumps of trees to be avoided, a child's footprint in ancient concrete in the far reaches of a large garden. They're in the names of lanes and roads, in decrepit old houses with barking dogs behind hedges over which you're too small to see. They hang ever-present in the air, you just *know* the stories are there – it's as natural and as normal as anything else in village life. You need only peer out from your bedroom window, across the fields to the gloom, to sense that *all is not what it seems.*

These tales make up a unique local history, woven through and connected by people, places and events, creating a super-narrow mythology – a circle of legends spanning a two- to three-mile diameter from the village centre, before reaching out like a fen Venn diagram whose edges overlap slightly with the next village's own stories. And so it continues, connecting settlement to settlement – via roads, bridges, and conversations over pints of ale in lonely pubs – to build a web of regional myth from the seed of hyper-local legends.

Some stories make it no further than the village boundary. These are *local tales for local people* – why you should stay away from the haunted house by the river with the big crack down the side, or avoid Elbow Lane at night due to the strange noises that waft across the fields at dusk. Outsiders have little need to heed such warnings – they wouldn't understand if you told them, so why bother trying?

Some stories, however, are so strange, so unsettling or so extraordinary that they effortlessly travel this timeless web of connections that link villages, extending out into the beyond, to be heard, processed and relayed by many more – and no doubt embellished in their journey through time and telling. Once enough people hear them, they begin to resonate a regional truth – and from that point on, they simply become as truthful as any word ever written, established and engrained.

THEY BECOME REAL.

I vividly remember my first experience in understanding the power of folk tales. I grew up in Parson Drove – a village deeply steeped in the fens, on the Cambridgeshire–Lincolnshire border. Back then and there, many of the hyper-local legends we simply absorbed. The house with the crack in it was haunted, and you could sometimes see the face of a lady behind a billowing curtain. If you walked around St John's Church three times anti-clockwise, then peered in through the window, you'd see the Devil. Cats had been nailed to that same church door as part of satanic rituals in years past. There was Holy Hannah, an old lady (*witch!*) who had walked from village to village, her hand bandaged in red cloth, claiming to have touched Christ – she would knock on doors and ask for food, before cursing the uncooperative occupants. Then, there was the house of a husband's murder-suicide, where you should pedal your bike double-speed when returning from tea at a friend's house. And of course, there was the ghost of Oliver Cromwell, aiming a cannon at the church from the mound behind the trees on Ghost Hill, halfway down the straight road to Murrow. These were just truths we all grew up with in our village.

Older kids would tell these stories to us down the park, or the setting would be up in the hayloft at my oldest friend Ben's place, where we'd camp out, play board games, and stay up far too late after exploring the near-pitch-black orchard. The time when folklore was seared into my brain was a dark night at the Spinney – an overgrown clump of trees standing alone in the gloom, beyond the bridge at the far end of the village, down a gravel track off Honey Corner, then down a further track and out into the fields.

The Spinney was a spooky place at the best of times. You had to go past a couple of old houses – occupants unknown – and far, far down a track. Once passed, and moving further down into the trees, there would always be remnants of a fire, and scraps of cloth and litter – unnerving clues that an *unknown someone* used this spot for shelter from time to time. It was an uneasy place – especially to a 10-year-old, as I was then.

Village kids hang around with whoever is about at any given time. Age seems less of a barrier in remote communities, maybe because your options are more limited. Whether it's playing football at the park, hanging out at the youth club, or just *hanging*, you end up interacting as a pack – whoever's there is there. This particular night there was a group of us down in the Spinney, making dens until dark. That's when the older kids start telling ghost stories. It's like a rite of passage: your time to get scared will come, your time to scare will come – and so goes the cycle.

On this one night, the older kids told us the story of a local woman who, a few years earlier – in the early 1980s – had walked the four sides of a block of fields surrounding the village. We all knew the route: through the village, up Sealey's Lane, turn left at the top, follow the river to Clough Bridge, back along the Village Green (past the house with the crack in it), and back to the village shop. Everyone knew the block – we'd often ride our bikes around it, I regularly fished the river near Clough Bridge. It was familiar. It was safe.

This poor woman had seen another side. By the time she reached the village store, she was visibly distressed, *shaking*. She told the shopkeeper how, as she'd walked along the river, she'd felt a presence following her. Glancing back, the woman had been startled by a huge, black, shaggy hound padding – slowly and silently, yet determinedly – just a short distance behind. It growled at her, and it glared at her through the malevolent ember of *its single glowing eye*. Terrified, the woman pulled up her hood and ran the remaining two miles or so, never once looking back.

The shopkeeper did her best to comfort the petrified woman, reassuring her that what she'd seen must have been a farmer's dog that had escaped – nothing to worry about. Yet she'd been *sure* it was something more sinister than that. Its size, its silence, its single glowing eye – she couldn't explain it, she just *knew* it was evil. Still, she'd had a lucky escape and was now back safe.

YET, EXACTLY ONE YEAR TO THE DAY OF THAT ENCOUNTER, WITH NO DISCERNABLE CAUSE, THE WOMAN DIED IN HER SLEEP. THERE WAS NO OTHER EXPLANATION: SHE'D BEEN CURSED BY BLACK SHUCK.

There, in the pitch-black and deathly fen silence, out in an isolated thicket of trees, amongst the undergrowth and gloom, I was frankly terrified. I remember some older kids laughing – maybe it *was* just a silly ghost story to them, maybe they just didn't believe it, maybe they just enjoyed scaring us. But to me, it meant something. We were talking about an inexplicable manifestation of *pure evil*, barely two miles from where we sat – a location so mundane, so familiar. Something so much a part of home, yet now the setting for something so dark, so otherworldly, so supernatural – and this terrible *'something'* existing beside and alongside our day-to-day reality. There, but not there. *Lurking.*

A VISION OF SHUCK WAS INDELIBLY BURNED INTO MY MEMORY, AND IT'S NEVER GONE AWAY.

I pedalled as hard as I could to get back home that night, but Shuck had sparked an interest in these type of tales that's only grown as I have. It sparked an interest in the stories, the landscape and the places – the connections of history, truth and legends with which East Anglia is so ripe. From the past to the present, we're surrounded by these tales, and they emerge from even the most unlikely places.

This book is a collection of some of my favourite stories from *these here parts* – some hyper-local, some having grown to become regional or even national truths. Whilst I've done my best to research as accurately as I can, and have walked and absorbed the locations where I've been able, will there be some exaggeration or certain inconsistencies when compared to other sources? No doubt. But that's part of the beauty of folklore – why stop a good story from being told? It's important to keep retelling these tales, and for different storytellers to tell them, thus keeping the tradition alive – a connection to our place, our past and ourselves is perhaps now more important than ever. If we knew where we were from, there'd be no doubt where we belong.

My one hope with all of this is to conjure in you a sense of dread and wonder similar to that which I felt as a 10-year-old boy upon first hearing about a hellhound in a dark fen woodland – and that you take these legends with you.

Keep your wits about you, folks. Out there be devils, dogs and demons. There, but not there. *Lurking.* Keep looking.

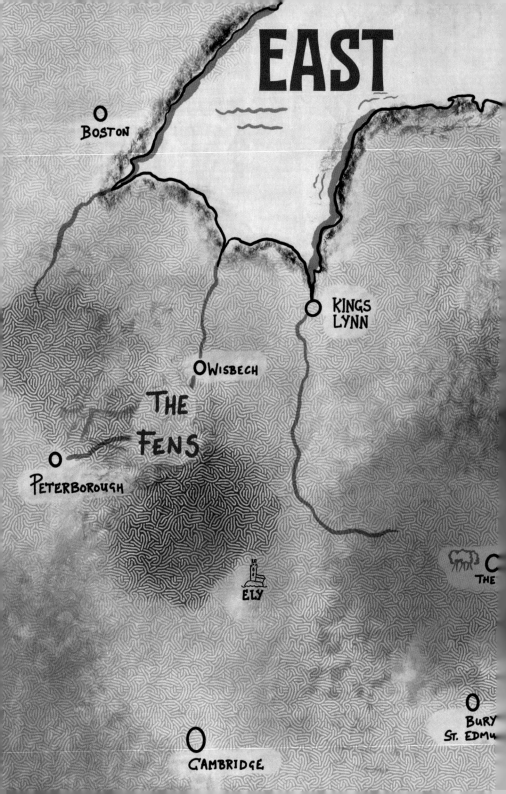

ANGLIA

CROMER

NORFOLK

NORWICH

GREAT
YARMOUTH

BUNGAY

SUFFOLK

Dunwich

Near **Watton** lies the wild and ancient **Wayland Wood**, scene of one of Norfolk's most tragic tales. First written about in **1595**, the now famous '**Babes in the Wood**' tells of two freshly orphaned children, a brother and sister whose fearful wails can still be heard echoing amongst the branches.

Upon the death of their father, and due a large inheritance, they were palmed off by a wicked uncle to two villianous rogues. The pair were employed to take the children to the woods and murder them so the uncle could lay claim to the family fortune.

No-one knows for sure what happened within those dark groves. Some say one rogue killed the other after an argument, then abandoned the children to starve. Some say he accomplished the gruesome task with a curved blade underneath a great oak.

ALL THAT IS KNOWN FOR SURE IS THAT THOSE CHILDREN NEVER RETURNED ALIVE.

Their bodies were eventually found under piles of leaves laid in place by the songbirds of the woods, nature respecting them where man had not.

The story is also connected to the scandal of **Robert de Grey of Merton Hall** who murdered his nephew to gain ownership of the vast manor house. Merton Hall lies to one edge of Wayland Wood and it is almost certain the cries of the de Grey child mingle with those emanating from deeper within.

Finally, the great oak beneath which the children lay dead was shattered by lightning in **1879**, adding a final exclaimation point to this most sorrowful story.

BABES
IN THE WOOD

THE BLACK DEATH ARRIVED IN NORFOLK IN 1348, DECIMATING THE POPULATION.

As a result of the misery and diminished workforce, life was hard for several decades. However, greedy landowners, barons and earls of rural communities still demanded that their fields be ploughed, and their livestock tended. With less people to work, the work was harder, but extra wages were not forthcoming. The people became restless.

This culminated in the **Peasants' Revolt of 1381**, when the common man rose up to remove the boot from their necks and began to rebel across the East.

In Norfolk the uprising was led by **Geoffrey Litster** who gathered a force and attacked several settlements in the county, including burning many buildings in Norwich. Eventually he and his motley army made camp in central Norfolk, just outside **North Walsham**. At the time, the Bishop of Norwich was **Henry le Despenser** who was away from Norfolk on an assignment in Rutland.

Upon receiving word of what was happening in his home county, Henry immediately raised a small force of highly trained knights and bowmen, and struck East through the Fens and Cambridgeshire, recruiting more men along the way.

EVENTUALLY THEY REACHED THE PEASANTS' CAMP, WHERE HENRY EARNT HIS MONIKER OF THE BATTLING BISHOP.

He himself led the charge. The peasants stood no chance. In fierce and brutal hand-to-hand combat, the peasants were massacred. Some retreated back to the town, but no respect was given to the sanctuary they had sought. Soon the Norfolk revolution was crushed, and their leader Litster was hung drawn and quartered in Norwich by le Despenser himself. There was no mistaking the peasants' place in the world, and where they should stay.

Henry le Despenser went on to lead crusades in Flanders, crush rebellions in Scotland, and be impeached. He died at his manor house in **North Elmham** and is buried in front of the high altar in Norwich Cathedral.

opposite page: Site of the Battle of North Walsham and ruins of Henry Le Despenser's manor house at North Elmham.
above: High altar at Norwich Cathedral, in front of which Le Despenser is buried.

ST FELIX OF BURGUNDY IS CREDITED WITH BRINGING CHRISTIANITY TO EAST ANGLIA
BUT HIS JOURNEY WAS NOT SMOOTH SAILING.

St Felix arrived in East Anglia from France by sea, sometime around **630AD**, having been despatched by the Roman **Honorius** to redeem the Anglo-Saxons from their pagan beliefs and lead them to embrace Christianity.

At the time the Wash was much larger, and much of the area in North West Norfolk (around **Kings Lynn and Sandringham**) was underwater, forming a much wider estuary than remains today. It was into this estuary and one of its tributaries, the **river Babingley**, that St Felix first attempted to strike land after his long journey at sea.

As he approached the river Babingley however, a fierce storm blew up – perhaps one final, defiant act by the pagan gods to resist their inevitable placation. St Felix was tossed and thrown in the waves, and his ship - already weathered and battered - began to sink. It was certain he would drown before being able to spread the word of the new Lord.

Yet suddenly from undergrowth along the river banks, a tribe of beavers appeared. Swimming out to Felix's stricken craft, and steadying it amongst the waves, they began building a bridge of logs for him to cross to the safety of the dry land. In this apparent miracle, he was saved physically - and now others could be spiritually.

In honour of this valiant rescue, Felix annointed the leader of the Beavers as the very first Bishop in East Anglia, and created the diocese of Babingley for the creature cleric to oversee. The brave beavers' actions are still commemorated on the village sign to this day.

St Felix then continued his journey across East Anglia, spreading Christianity as he went until founding a church in **Dunmoc** (modern day **Dunwich**, the vast majority of which has been lost to the sea), where he reigned as Archbishop of East Anglia. He died in around 647. His corpse was moved to Soham, later to be desecrated by Vikings. His relics (remains) were later stolen by the monks of **Ramsey Abbey** in the thick mist of a fenland night, the motivation being to boost the abbey's potential as a pilgrimage destination from their nearby rival abbey at Ely.

THE BEAVER BISHOP
OF BABINGLEY

ON THE FATEFUL EVENING OF 4TH AUGUST 1577, EAST ANGLIAN FOLKLORE WAS CHANGED FOREVER.

As a terrible storm raged outside, the parishoners of St Mary's church in **Bungay, Suffolk** sheltered fearfully inside, praying to God to keep them safe. As rain lashed down and fearsome winds howled, their prayers were indeed heeded... but by an altogether different entity than the one they hoped for.

Thunder boomed and lightning cracked, striking the church tower with violent force. As the roof caved in, and rubble and timbers fell from above, the doors flung open. There - savage, snarling, smoking - stood **Black Shuck.**

THE HELLHOUND.

He tore through the congregation, wringing the necks of several with his fearsome claws. The intense heat radiating from him caused several other worshippers to shrivel up like burnt leather purses. He launched and tore the priest limb from limb right there at the altar. Destruction wrought aplenty, he turned and bounded into the night, and into the psyche of East Anglia forevermore. That same night, he appeared at **Blythburgh** church, his claws searing burn marks in the door as fearful villagers barricaded it shut. His marks are still visible to this day.

Since then, and for over 400 years, this beast has stalked the land, roaming the North Norfolk Coast, the isolated fens, and beyond. Descriptions of Shuck differ - sometimes he has a single eye, sometimes two, sometimes he has no head at all.

He's been known to guide lonely travellers to safety, to patrol the coast in search of shipwrecks, but most often is a harbinger of fear and doom - a terrible and terrifying beast who may kill you now, or mark you for death within a year. He may even be the Devil himself.

BE CAREFUL, MY FRIENDS, FOR WHEREVER YOU MAY WANDER, OLD SHUCKE MAY BE AWAITING.

"HE TAKES THE FORM OF A HUGE BLACK DOG, AND PROWLS ALONG DARK LANES AND LONESOME FIELD FOOTPATHS, WHERE, ALTHOUGH HIS HOWLING MAKES THE HEARER'S BLOOD RUN COLD, HIS FOOTFALLS MAKE NO SOUND. YOU MAY KNOW HIM AT ONCE, SHOULD YOU SEE HIM, BY HIS FIERY EYE; HE HAS BUT ONE, AND THAT, LIKE THE CYCLOPS', IS IN THE MIDDLE OF HIS HEAD. BUT SUCH AN ENCOUNTER MIGHT BRING YOU THE WORST OF LUCK: IT IS EVEN SAID THAT TO MEET HIM IS TO BE WARNED THAT YOUR DEATH WILL OCCUR BEFORE THE END OF THE YEAR."

Opposite page: a footpath close to Blythburgh, site of many Black Shuck sightings

opposite page: Blythburgh Church and Shuck's claw marks burnt into the door.
above: Blythburgh village sign.

The dramatic ruins of **St Andrews Church** in **Covehithe** on the Suffolk Coast...

...said to be haunted by the **Faceless Lady**

THE SPECTRE OF OLIVER CROMWELL LOOMS LARGE OVER EAST ANGLIA

From his childhood home in **Ely,** and his role as governer of that same city, to the bombardment of **Crowland Abbey** in the Civil War to oust the Royalist troops garrisioned within, to smaller isolated stories across the landscape such as Cromwell's ghostly troops and spectral cannon aimed at St John's church from **Ghost Hill** between the remote villages of **Parson Drove and Murrow**, you are never far from a story about Cromwell in East Anglia.

YET THE STRANGEST STORY OF ALL CONCERNS HIS SEVERED HEAD.

Following his brutal but victorious Civil War campaign, and the execution of his opponent King Charles I, Cromwell ruled as Lord Protector of the British Isles from **1653** until his death from blood poisoning (related to an urinary infection) in 1658. He was given a huge state funeral, and was suceeeded by his son. By 1661 however, the Protectorate had failed under his inept leadership, and King Charles II was reinstated as ruler. The Royalists had long and bitter memories.

Cromwell's body was exhumed, tried, and given a posthoumus execution by beheading. It took eight blows to sever his head, which was then impaled on a spike and displayed atop Westminster Hall. However, a few days later, it disappeared.

It is thought that a guard picked up the head and stashed it in his chimney at home. It was later seen displayed in a London museum belonging to Claudius Du Puy, but upon his death it went missing again. Discovered several years later on a market stall, the gnarly noggin was purchased and thereafter exhibited at various freakshows and oddity fayres. Many sales, exhibitions and counterfeits later, the head made its way to **Sidney Sussex College in Cambridge**, where Cromwell had studied. It was encased in a sturdy oak box and buried in a secret location on the college grounds in 1960.

You may have thought this would have brought Cromwell peace at last, but you would be wrong. His toothless and scarred head - still run through by its iron spike - now regularly floats around the chambers and corridors of Sidney Sussex College, screaming and searching for serene slumber.

THE DISEMBODIED HEAD

OF OLIVER
CROMWELL

Berney Brograve is one of Norfolk's most legendary characters - a land-owning, fist-fighting, smuggler-bashing lord with many tales told about his exploits.

For this particular story, we'll take ourselves back to **1771**, deep in the marsh near Horsey Mere. It was here where, in order to obtain the right to drain the land using the mill he had built a few years prior, Black Hearted Berney entered a wager with the Devil himself...

The contest was to see who could mow a nearby field the fastest. If Berney won, he could drain the the land with impunity; if the Devil triumphed, his prize would be nothing less than Berney's soul.

THE DEVIL WON WITH EASE.
And one dark and windy night, he soon returned to collect his prize.

Berney, exhibiting the scandalous and beligerent behaviour he was renowned for, had no intention of surrendering his soul to Satan. As the winds howled and rains crashed down, he barricaded himself within the mill, where the Devil could not enter.

For the whole night, the demon crashed and bashed against the mill. He **huffed and he puffed** at its sails, and pounded on the doors. All the while, Berney cowered inside, somewhat regretting his choices.

As the sun rose, the Devil departed and Berney dared to peek outside. The damage was considerable - the mill leaned westward where the Devil had tried to topple it over; its walls were pockmarked with cloven hoofprints.

This is how the mill remains - a solitary, shattered sentinel looming over the marsh. And on dark and stormy nights, you can be sure the Devil returns to check in...

TO CLAIM ANY SOULS, AND SETTLE HIS DEBT.

DEVIL'S

WINDMILL

The village of **Geldeston** is remote and picturesque, with lovely walks along the banks of the river Waveney heading in both directions from the village centre. However, this quiet and quaint community hides one of the most concentrated collection of creepy capers anywhere in the East.

Whether it is **Blunderhazard of Barsham Hall**, who every Christmas drives his spectral carriage full pelt across the fields to **Norwich**, or the skeleton of a wicked criminal chained to a stone at the bottom of the village pond and whose spirit wanders the village at night, moaning and clanking his chains. There is even a **ghostly donkey** that haunts the fields just beyond the village boundary.

But... of all Geldeston's spirits, none is more sinister or terrifying than the one that haunts the narrow lanes around the churchyard that meet at a junction known as the **Gelders**. It is here that you might encounter a shapeless, shifting shadow - it might be as small as a dog, or as large as a horse; it's something that can never truly be focused on, but be sure... it's there.

How it looks is hard to pin down. Any unfortunate witnesses have all described it differently, but how it *feels* is never in doubt, for that is the same every time. If, when strolling those lanes in rain or shine, bright midday sun or darkest night, you feel an overwhelming and claustrophobic sense of dread and terror, make no mistake - and if you make it home, be grateful - for you have encountered THE HATEFUL THING.

Geldeston's picturesque walks belie the village's many sinister secrets.

HATEFUL

THING

HEREWARD THE WAKE WAS A SCOURGE OF THE NORMANS AND A FENLAND THORN IN THE SIDE OF WILLIAM THE CONQUERER.

Born in **Bourne, Lincolnshire in 1035**, at age 18 he was declared an outlaw and sent into exile. Whilst travelling around his adventures included slaying a giant bear in Cornwall, rescuing a princess and fighting as a mercenary in Flanders.

Hearing of the Norman invasion of England in 1066, Hereward returned home to find his family slaughtered and his brother's head on a pike. He vowed revenge.

Having enlisted a small band of feared fen fighting men such as **Leofine the Scythe**, **Wulric the Heron**, and the 'Robber of Drayton' - and wielding his trusty sword, **Brain-biter** - he established a secret base deep within the fens from which to launch guerilla attacks on the oppressors before melting back into the mists and marshes. To reassure the local peasants, he split a goose feather into four and sent messengers to each corner of the fens with the message:

"THE WAKE IS COMING."

Hereward and his small army claimed many victories: slaughtering many Normans throughout the East, killing 15 drunken knights in Bourne and sacking Peterborough abbey. Eventually he founded a stronghold on the **Isle of Ely** from which to defend the area. This became the scene of his most famous victory.

As William the Conquerer's forces amassed to assault the city, Hereward and some witches he had enlisted set fire to the reed beds of the marshes behind them, trapping them on their hastily constructed wooden bridge. The bridge sank under the weight of their armour, drowning them all and saving the city.

A few nights later however, the Normans bribed a monk of Ely to show them safe passage through the miserable marshes to ambush Hereward. For a time, he and his men escaped, rowing through the fens via Upwell. Yet Hereward was eventually caught and slain, and his body later taken to rest at Crowland Abbey.

His legend has lived on though, as an inspiration to freedom fighters, including no less than the legendary Robin Hood and certainly the fearsome bands of Fen Tigers who later fought efforts to drain the marshland.

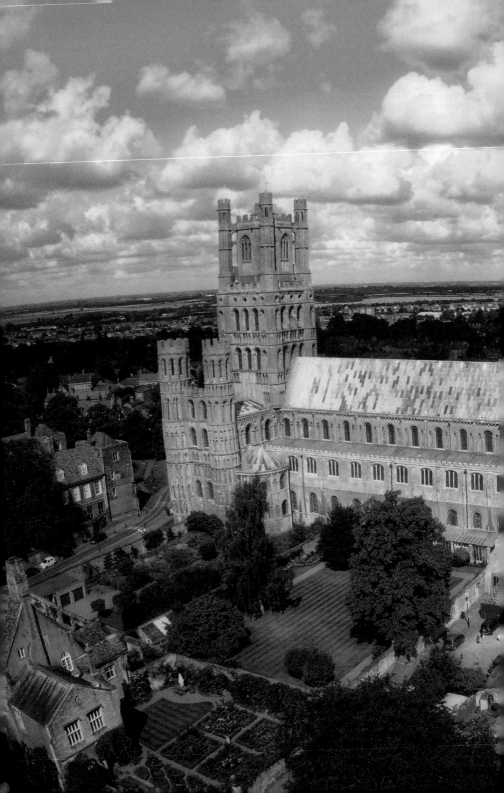

GURGUNT

THE KING UNDER THE MOUND

Norwich Castle is a Norman keep, situated on a fortified mound in the very centre of the 'Fine City'. However, its history reaches back far beyond the Normans and into the distant pre-Roman times.

Way back in those dark eras of conflict and superstition, a king named **Gurgunt** ruled East Anglia. Upon his death, he was buried deep with the castle mound - sat upon his throne, surrounded by his treasures, with his sword in hand.

HE REMAINS THERE TO THIS DAY.

However, rumour has it that in fact he did not die at all, but actually remains deep in slumber ready to be awoken if the city of Norwich ever needs his assistance in an hour of desperate need.

King John is one of England's most reviled regal reprobates. A brutal and incompetent king known for oppressing, taxing and starving his subjects, he was feared throughout the land. However, the land itself did not fear him, especially the boggy mudflats around the estuary of **the Wash** - a large bay that cuts into both Norfolk and Lincolnshire, where East Anglia connects with the rest of the country.

Whilst struck down with dysentry on a visit to **Kings Lynn** in **October 1216**, John decided to head to **Swineshead Abbey** near Boston to recover. While he and his retinue took the longer but firmer route via Wisbech, he sent his baggage train containing all of his jewels and treasure via a shorter, but much more perilous route across the fens.

As his caravan approached the River Nene, near to present day **Sutton Bridge**, it slowly began to cross the muddy flats of the estuary. The fens were not going to let the tyrant's crimes and arrogance go unpunished! The deep mud began to clog the wheels of the wagons, sucking them down and preventing them from completing the fording of the river.

SOON THE INEVITABLE TIDE ROSE, SWALLOWING THE RICHES, NEVER TO BE SEEN AGAIN!

King John died of his ailments soon after - and even 800 years later, no trace of his fortune has ever been uncovered. There are thoughts that it may have been an insurance job, or that the caravan was a mere diversion and he had really hidden his treasure in Kings Lynn to keep it from his enemies. Some say a local farmer became immensely rich overnight but refused to explain how.

I, however, believe that only the fens themselves know the secret: they claimed the king's wealth for their own, and it still lies deep beneath the silt, never to corrupt another man again.

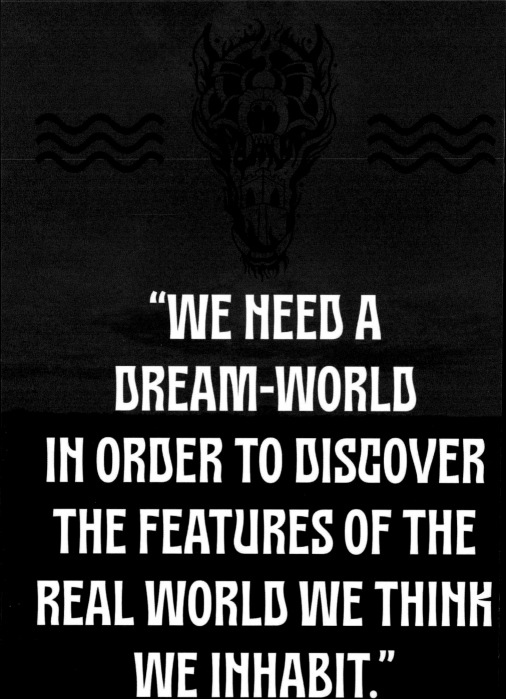

"WE NEED A DREAM-WORLD IN ORDER TO DISCOVER THE FEATURES OF THE REAL WORLD WE THINK WE INHABIT."

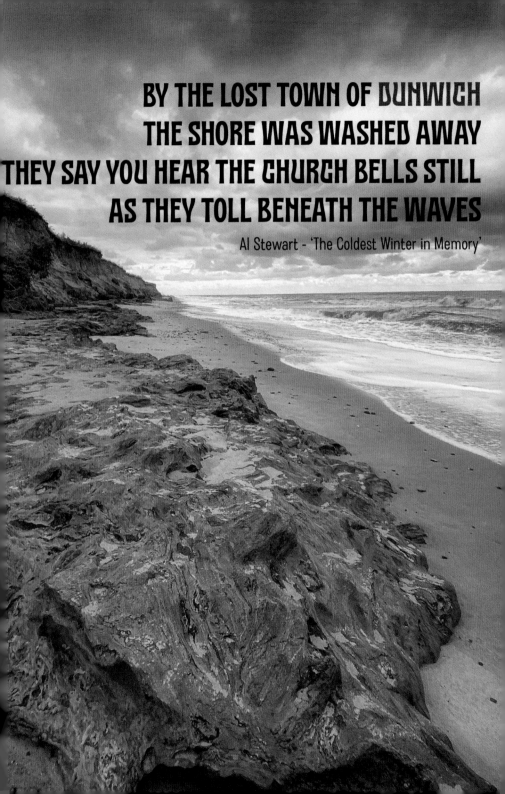

BY THE LOST TOWN OF DUNWICH
THE SHORE WAS WASHED AWAY
THEY SAY YOU HEAR THE CHURCH BELLS STILL
AS THEY TOLL BENEATH THE WAVES

Al Stewart - 'The Coldest Winter in Memory'

The Fens are a difficult terrain to navigate: dark misty marshes with limited and treacherous routes through the bog. If you find yourself lost out in those lonely wetlands, you may be tempted to follow flickering, comforting lights out in the reeds.... Resist at all costs!

Those lights are not beacons to guide you to the safety of dry land... they are the **Lantern Men** of the fens!

MALEVOLENT FENLAND SPIRITS, TRYING TO LURE YOU TO A DARK AND DISMAL DEMISE.

It is said they are especially prevalent in the area around **Wicken Fen** and are known to be attracted by the sound of idle whistling.

If you do sense them nearby, then the only way to resist their lure is to throw yourself face down into the mud with your mouth agape. They will then float harmlessly over you in search of a less informed wetland wanderer to seduce.

Be careful out there!

In **1782**, the quiet village of **Ludham** found itself embroiled in one of the strangest stories in Norfolk folklore.

A hole appeared on the main street, close to the village pub, which upon closer inspection by the curious villagers was found to lead to an underground maze of tunnels stretching far beneath the churchyard and beyond. These were no ordinary tunnels, however - they had been dug by a **dragon** that had made its lair beneath the sleepy village.

Every day the villagers blocked the entrance to the tunnels with rubble, but every night the creature broke through to terrorise the village, savage the local livestock, and generally cause all sorts of mayhem. Soon, no-one would leave their house after dark.

DESCRIBED AS A 'SUPRISING REPTILE', IT WAS SAID TO MEASURE A FULL 15 FEET LONG, WINGED AND SCALED, WITH A FEARSOME MOUTH FILLED WITH RAZOR SHARP TEETH. IT RESEMBLED A DRAGON OR MONSTROUS SERPENT. IT BECAME KNOWN AS THE LUDHAM WORM.

The villagers were powerless against it. Each day they blocked the hole, each night it burst through to run rampant around the parish. Over time, the worm grew in confidence until eventually, one bright summers day, it flagrantly mocked the villagers by leaving its lair in broad daylight, stretching out on the vilage green to bask in the warmth of the afternoon sun.

As most villagers cowered inside with fear, one brave and enterprising man seized his moment. Whilst the worm snoozed arrogantly in the sun, the villager heaved a single huge boulder from the far end of the village to the entrance of the serpent's lair. Using all of his strength, he rolled it into place, blocking the entrance forever.

Upon awakening and attemping to return underground - only to find its home blocked off - the worm became enraged. With a reptilian roar and thrashing of its tail, the worm damaged several buildings in the village before heading across the fields to nearby **St Benets Abbey** where, with one final lash of its tail it struck the abbey walls. As masonry fell around it, it entered the vaults beneath St Benets and plunged once more underground, **never to be seen again**.

THE GREATEST EVIL EVER TO STALK EAST ANGLIA WAS NOT A DEMON, GHOST NOR BEAST.
IT WAS A MAN.

The years between **1644** and **1647** are some of the darkest England has ever experienced, and East Anglia was central to the distrust, superstition and sheer terror that blanketed the land, for those few short years were when notorious Witchfinder **Matthew Hopkins** and his associate **John Stearne** stalked the realm.

Born in **Great Wenham**, Suffolk, in around 1620 - the son of a puritan priest - and into a land torn apart by civil war, the situation was ripe for Hopkins to capitalise o fear and suspicion amongst the small towns and villages of the remote East, and capitalise he indeed did.

Proclaiming himself a virtuous man in the service of the Lord in his duty of uncovering witches, he and Stearne travelled the land from settlement to settlement, convincing councils to pay him vast sums to uncover witches' covens i their parishes. Hopkins focused mainly on Suffolk and Norfolk, whilst Stearne travelled a parallel route through Cambridgeshire and the Fens.

Mere whispers or rumours were enough for him to seize poor women, young and ol They were then imprisoned, brutally tortured through sleep deprivation, pricked wi sharp instruments and of course cast into rivers to see if they would float or drow Once their inevitable guilt had been determined, Hopkins gleefully executed them e masse through hanging or burning. As he wrote himself:

"EVERY OLD WOMAN WITH A WRINKLED FACE, A FURROWED BROW, A HAIRY LIP, A ROBBER TOOTH, A SQUINT EYE, A SQUEAKING VOICE OR SCOLDING TONGUE, HAVING A RUGGED COAT ON HER BACK, A SKULL CAP ON HER HEAD, A SPINDLE IN HER HAND & A DOG OR CAT BY HER SIDE, I NOT ONLY SUSPECT BUT PRONOUNCED FOR A WITCH"

His reign as Witchfinder was short but brutal. It is recorded that he was responsib for the deaths of as many as **300 poor souls in just 3 years**, including the largest ever single witch trial held in **Bury St Edmunds** - more than had been executed in the previous 100 years combined - with his name thereafter becoming synonymou with evil forevermore.

MATTHEW HOPKINS
WITCHFINDER GENERAL
& EVIL INCARNATE

NORFOLK NOWHERES

There are approximately **200 deserted or abandoned settlements in Norfolk**, where, for the most part, nothing remains other than signs in the dirt. Marks of streets, foundations, earthworks, and often a striking church ruin are all that remain where once people lived and worked.

These settlements were all abandoned for a multitude of reasons: failing crops, landowners seizing the property to add to their estate, and the Black Death hitting a population so hard it could not recover. The 3 locations on these pages are examples of each of these causes for abandonment.

This page: **Roudham** church ruins overlooking the site of the old village, which was ravaged by plague in **1349**. However, there was a stable population until the 1700s - until the church was nearly destroyed by fire in **1736**.

Opposite page (top and inset): Aerial shot of one of the most famous lost Norfolk villages, **Godwick**. A series of bad harvests caused villagers to leave around **1428**, and the population never recovered. The streets are clearly visible from above. Unfortunately the church tower was covered in scaffolding on my visit.

Opposite page (bottom): **Bawsey** church ruins, all that is left of a settlement demolished in the 16th Century by a greedy landowner who evicted the residents and turned their home into farmland.

NORTH CREAKE ABBEY

Sent into ruin by Plague, which killed all of the resident monks in **1506.**

In **1528,** a treasure-hunting monk by the name of **William Stapleton** conducted necromantic rituals here in the hope of resurrecting the departed souls to tell him where the abbey's lost treasure was hidden.

One night in **1765**, two farmers making their way home after a day's toil in the fields around **Happisburgh** were terrified to find themselves with a gruesome companion.

Just ahead of them floated an apparition of a sailor, but one with severed legs and his decapitated head resting down his back, hanging by a thread of skin. The nautical nightmare clutched a sack, and as the farmers followed in awe, the spectre eventually reached the village well, into which it floated down into and disappeared.

The next day, after hearing the farmers' tale, the villagers decided to investigate the well, and using a grappling hook retrieved two sacks from its murky depths.

ONE SACK CONTAINED THE HEADLESS TORSO OF A SAILOR WITH A PISTOL TUCKED IN ITS BELT; THE OTHER, A PAIR OF BOOTS WITH SOME HAIRY FEET STILL INSIDE.

Noticing blood spatters around the well, the villagers followed the trail of blood stains to a secluded area of beach near **Cart Gap** where broken bottles, blood and a discarded pistol highlighted a fierce and fatal fight between the freshly spectral sailor and a gang of North Norfolk brandy smugglers.

After this initial encounter, the phantom began appearing regularly - and every night, wailing and moaning would emanate from the bottom of the well.

In truth, the only thing that stopped the hauntings and terrible moaning was the eventual capping of the well with a pump, ensuring this sea-faring spirit would forever be known as the **Pump Hill Spectre.**

PUMP HILL SPECTRE

HAPPISBURGH LIGHTHOUSE

Constructed from huge rocks, the world famous Stonehenge in Wiltshire is a prehistoric site of great importance that has stood for several thousand years. It provides a window into the deepest British history and will no doubt continue to inspire and inform for thousands more years to come.

The East lacks such megaliths due to the scarcity of suitable stone to provide lasting memorials to our ancestors. However, that does not mean the Neolithic people of East Anglia did not build monuments of equal gravitas and importance, as the discovery of **Seahenge** in **1998** by **John Lorimer** in the saltmarshes of **Holme-next-the-Sea** proves.

Lorimer first discovered an axe-head buried out in the marsh, and quickly spotted a timber pillar exposed by the tide-shifted sands. Further excavation uncovered a circular structure nearly 7 metres wide, and 3 metres high, constructed from 55 oak pillars sunk and preserved in the silt. In the centre of the circle was a vast oak stump, buried upside down with its roots splayed out to form a platform, or perhaps an altar. Carbon dating shows that it was constructed out in the marsh, where sea meets land, in the summer of **2049 BC**. Tool marks show that at least 50 people were involved in its construction.

Its purpose remains unknown, as no written records exist. Was it a site of ritual and worship to the gods of salt, sea and sky? One of the more compelling theories is that the upturned oak provided a crossing point into the afterlife for important figures and other leaders of the North Norfolk tribes. The trunk itself may have provided a passage to the underworld, or the platform formed by the roots may have elevated the spirit skyward.

It is known that a common method of burial for significant figures in that era was the practice of **excarnation**, where the body is lain open to the elements, and slowly defleshed by birds who carry the soul upwards to the heavens. It is likely that Seahenge was reserved for this purpose for the most revered tribal elders.

Whatever the purpose, it is clear this was a site of great importance to prehistoric East Anglians, and it is likely that the area was rich with such monuments that have unfortunately fallen prey to time and rot.

Much to the disgust of modern druids, the Seahenge site was excavated, and removed to ensure its preservation, and is now visitable in **Kings Lynn museum**.

SEAHENGE

Much of Norfolk is pitted with shallow holes, either dry or filled with water. It's said that many contain treasure, often in the form of golden gates. Some were used as ambush spots by highwaymen who now haunt these pits; some contain the dead from viking battles; some are entrances to Hell itself. However, the particular holes around **Aylmerton and Northrepps** - close to Sheringham on the North Norfolk coast - are known as **The Shrieking Pits**.

LOCATIONS OF LOSS AND DESPAIR THAT RESONATE THROUGH THE CENTURIES.

Both of these villages are close to each other, and both have pits in the fields around them, both areas have tales of sorrow and pain, but there are distinct differences.

In **Northrepps**, the pits are the location where Esmerelda, a young village girl, threw herself into the depths after becoming besotted with a local farmer. When their short but passionate affair was discovered and the local clergyman put an end to it, the grief stricken Esmerelda decided to commit suicide and flung herself into the deepest hollow. She changed her mind, but too late -she cried for help, but no-one came to her rescue. Her cries are still heard every **February 24th**, the anniversary of her demise.

Nearby in **Aylmerton**, where a cluster of pits lie close together, an even sadder legend prevails. Here, believing a baby not to be his, a jealous husband murdered his own child and threw the body into one of the perilous pits. No-one has ever identified exactly which one.

Returning from his grisly task, the man then also murdered his wife. Indeed, it is her spirit, tormented by the incomprehensible grief, that haunts this area - fruitlessly searching for her child in each of the pits in turn, and wailing in sorrow as she is inevitably disappointed time and time again. Her mournful howls can still be heard floating across the countryside as far as **Weybourne**.

SHRIEKING
PITS OF NORTHREPPS
AND AYLMERTON

The Fens has many notorious families whose names are known throughout the marsh, mostly through acts of criminality and violence. Pick a fight with one and you pick a fight with them all, Soon, the clan descends without mercy, claiming retribution in either property or wounding. Yet no other family has struck more fear across the wetlands than the terrifying **Sierbert brothers of Shippea Hill.**

In a remote farmhouse in **Sedge Fenn** - close to a trackway across some of the remotest fens and leading all the way from **Thorney to Hockwold** - lived six hulking brothers; far larger, stronger and scarier than ordinary men.

AT LEAST THEY WERE THOUGHT TO BE MEN, AS NO-ONE WHO EVER SAW THEM UP CLOSE LIVED TO SHARE THEIR DESCRIPTIONS.

As travellers journeyed along the trackway, the brothers would attack with extreme violence, dragging their victims back to their farmhouse where no doubt further untold horrors were delivered upon these poor souls.

All any witnesses ever saw were six huge, shambling shadows in the mist - each carrying a body with them back into the swamp. A choir of agonised screams rang nightly across Sedge Fenn with each group of victims in turn adding to the cacophony.

The brothers claimed so many victims that when this area of the fens was drained in the early 19th Century, revealing countless skeletons, it became known as **The Bone Yard.**

Whilst the trackway has fallen out of use for the most part, if you ever happen to be walking in that area, keep your wits about you. If you see a party of six men approaching, turn on your heel and run as fast as you can, or the only fate that awaits is becoming a resident of the infamous Sierbert cemetery of silt.

FOR A THOUSAND YEARS, ST BENETS ABBEY HAS STOOD PROMINENT AND STEADFAST OVER THE NORFOLK MARSHES.

A thousand years is a long time, and this abbey has a storied history and many tales. It was founded in the 9th Century on a site next to the River Bure. Here, the hermit Suneman made his home, and was later murdered by invading Danes. St Benets has survived disasters - both natural flooding and man made, such as a siege by Canute - and was the location of the last sighting of the **Ludham Worm** (covered elsewhere in this book). However, its darkest tale is that of **Essric the Traitor**, a monk who oversaw the gates at St Benets around the time of the Norman Conquest.

As William the Conquerer's forces made their way through England, it was inevitable they would eventually reach Norfolk, and of course St Benets Abbey itself. They laid siege to the abbey, but the walls were strong, and the prudent abbot had ensured healthy stockpiles of food and supplies. The Normans could not crack the will of the monks, nor their defences.

But Essric was ambitious, and weak. He could see a path to respect and authority. He snuck away from the abbey one dark night and into the Norman camp, offering to open the abbey doors for them in return for the prize he desired...being annointed as Abbot himself. The Normans gladly took him up on his proposal, and he unlocked the gates. The Normans did not hesitate, soon rampaging through the abbey and taking it over. Essric got his prize, but with much blood of his brother monks on his hands.

The Normans granted a huge procession for Essric's coronation - and dressed in full regalia, he relished the occasion. However, the Normans had no intention of letting such a deceitful figure oversee such an important asset.

THE BETRAYER BECAME THE BETRAYED.

Just as the coronation was nearing completion, the Normans seized Essric, stripped him first of his robes, and then after nailing him to the very same doors he had opened for them, stripped him of his skin as well. His shrieks cut across the marshes on that night, and have done every **May 25th** since then, when his spirit is seen writhing and wriggling in agonising pain for eternity.

ews of St Benets Abbey as it now stands. The large tower is the ruin of an old windmill installed into
e previous gatehouse by a farmer in the 18th Century.

NOT MUCH IS KNOWN ABOUT THE LIFE OF EDMUND, KING OF EAST ANGLIA, BUT HIS DEATH RESONATES THROUGH THE AGES.

Crowned in **855**, his reign was defined by ongoing wars with the savage viking raiders, led by **Ivar the Boneless.**

After rampaging and pillaging through East Anglia, it is said that the Heathen Army eventually caught up with Edmund in the village of **Hoxne** on **20th November 870**.

Outnumbered by a superior, more battle-hardened enemy, Edmund fought bravely, but was captured, tied to a tree, tortured and shot through with arrows.

Finally, refusing to renounce Christ, he was beheaded and his head thrown into a nearby wood. As his men searched for it, a luminescent talking wolf led them to its location, guiding them by growling "Here...here... *HERE.*"

It was retrieved as safely as a disembodied head can be. Miraculously, whilst being placed on top of his neck in preparation for burial, Edmund's head fused itself back onto his body and sealed the wound shut. Thusly, he was venerated as a Saint.

His remains were laid to rest in the nearby town of **Bury**, which took his name as a result. Many other locations throughout Norfolk also lay claim to the site of his martyrdom, therefore making Edmund the true saint of all East Anglia.

WARRIOR, MONK, AND FINALLY,
HERMIT.

ST. GUTHLAC

After a full life of travel and battle, St. Guthlac finally moved to a remote island deep within the fens to live a solitary existence of worship and ritual.

He wore no wool, linen or any soft garments; he ate no food but barley bread and muddy water. He suffered from marsh fever and was regularly troubled by visions of vile demons.

When he died, Guthlac exhaled nectar, and angels sang as his soul departed and rose to the sky in a beam of light. His body never decayed.

A fenland cult in his honour was formed and grew over time, eventually resulting in the establishment of **Crowland abbey** in the 8th Century on the site of his lonely island home.

TRULY THE SAINT OF THE FENS.

The ruins of Crowland Abbey - founded by the Cult of St. Guthlac and built upon the fenland island where he retreated to live the life of a hermit.

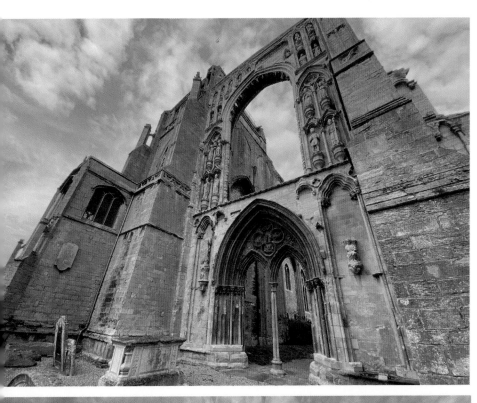

The salt marshes of the **North Norfolk Coast** have long provided its villages and hamlets with bountiful harvests and sustenance from the sea.

Whether gathering the samphire, or collecting shellfish, villagers have trekked out into the area where marshes meet the sea for centuries. Not all have returned.

For years, the village of **Stiffkey** was renowned for the quality of its cockles, and for the determination of the women who collected them - known as the '**StiffKey Amazons**'.

A tough, back-breaking task, and a race against the tide, cockling relies on you making it out to the far reaches of the saltflats, collecting as many of the briny bivalves as you can, then carrying your bulging sacks back to firm ground before the marsh is swallowed by the sea once more.

One fateful day, with her rent due, an unfortunate cockler named **Nancy** stayed behind, long after her fellow amazons had headed home, to try and fill one last sack of shellfish before the sea returned.

TIME AND TIDE SHOWED NO MERCY, AND NANCY WAS DEVOURED BY FROTH AND FOG.

Although her body was eventually recovered, her spirit will never rest. She remains out on the mudlfats to this day, screaming in the mists every night there's a storm like the one that consumed her.

KING RAEDWALD

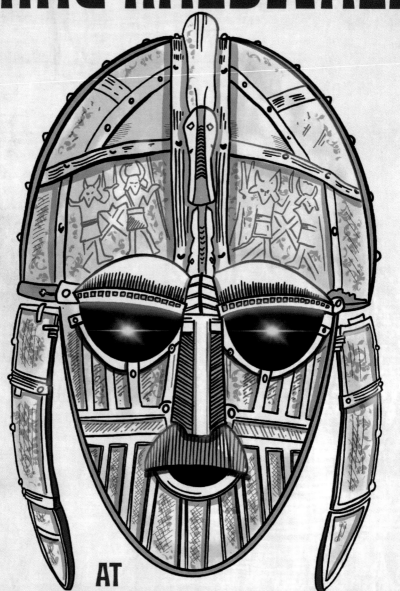

AT SUTTON HOO

EAST ANGLIA IS HOME TO THE GREATEST TREASURE EVER DISCOVERED IN THE BRITISH ISLES. SITUATED IN AN AREA AROUND WOODBRIDGE IN SUFFOLK, IT IS KNOWN AS THE ENGLISH VALLEY OF KINGS.

HERE AT SUTTON HOO, AMONGST BURIAL MOUNDS OF SAXON NOBLES, THE SHIP BURIAL OF RAEDWALD - THE MOST POWERFUL RULER OF EAST ANGLIA - WAS DISCOVERED.

Whilst not much is known of early East Anglian history due to the pillage and destruction of written records by marauding viking raiders in the 9th Century, Raedwald was so powerful that most of his story has prevailed throughout the ages.

Born into the Wuffinga dynasty, Raedwald reigned over the kingdom of East Anglia from **599 until 624**. In the later part of his reign, he was known as the most powerful English king south of the River Humber.

Amongst Raedwald's more notable achievements were holding the only royal Christian shrine in England, and defeating the Northumbrians and therefore seizing control of the majority of the country at the Battle of the River Idle. He also founded the town of **Gipeswic (Ipswich)** and oversaw much of its early development into a bustling port.

He died around 624 and was buried, along with his ship and hoards of treasure, in the barrows at **Sutton Hoo**, close to the River Deben in Suffolk. His grave was discovered in 1939 - luckily still intact, having been narrowly missed by early grave robbers who had pillaged the other mounds.

The treasures included the ship itself (one of only 2 ship burials ever discovered in England), hoards of jewellery and silverware, an incredible sceptre of power, and most famously **Raedwald's helmet** itself - an even more ancient artifact, carved with imagery of dragons and dancing warriors.

No-one truly knows the extent of his power, but the fact that his burial mound contained such items and he was honoured in such a magnificent way is enough to strengthen his claim as East Anglia's one true king.

East Anglia is often dismissed as lacking in scenery. It's seen as flat and featureless – nothing but fen, field and farmland. Functional – there to supply the rest of the country with wheat and root vegetables. More often than not, it's skipped as a holiday destination in favour of the Highlands, the Lake District or the undulating coasts of Cornwall and Devon.

I believe East Anglia is actually one of the most varied areas in the country. Colossal fenland skies, where huge clouds and weather systems move slowly through, viewed without obstruction. It's as if you're stood in the centre of a flat-bottomed glass dome with the universe itself painting on its surface. Standing on an ancient island visible for miles, the Isle of Ely and the Cathedral were used as landmarks in bygone times, to navigate through the murky marshes. Then there's the North Norfolk coast, hosting some of the country's finest beaches – stretching unbroken for around a hundred miles from Hunstanton to Great Yarmouth, interspersed with mysterious silt and salt marshes, and seal colonies. Inland, you'll find the Norfolk broads – a waterway maze meandering and connecting through woods, villages and marshes, with old pumping mills standing guard over them like sentinels. Further East still is the Suffolk coast – very much gentrified in many places, yet still desolate and strange, where towns such as Dunwich have been washed from the cliffs and into the waves over the course of centuries. On the Norfolk and Suffolk border lies Thetford Forest, where the pine trees stand tall, and the soil underfoot is sandy in comparison to the claggy Mid-Norfolk clay – you can feel like you're walking through sand dunes at times, despite being at least an hour from the coast in any direction.

There are also the interspersed villages, towns and cities. Flint cottages provide a distinct and uniquely East Anglian identity to every small village green or coastal road, while the regional centres of Norwich and Cambridge – modern cities – still reveal their prehistory and medieval origins.

Most importantly, though, East Anglia *feels* different. The landscape and the stories that make up this book are completely intertwined, and this is a concept that fascinates me. On our many walks around the region (both for pleasure and to research the locations of the tales found in this book), there's an undeniable language of the land, stories from the soil – and you can *feel* it. It's truly a beautiful part of the world: on a summer's day, walking through a field of wheat, warm yellow above and around you – it's a special, tranquil feeling that I simply don't experience anywhere else. But there's also a weirdness I don't feel anywhere else, with that sense of weirdness differing even across those distinct areas within East Anglia. And all of this seems simultaneously informed and enhanced by the stories that originate from there.

Take the Devil, for example: he has appeared most often in the villages around Acle, just before the marshes that reach out toward Great Yarmouth. In those historic times, the marshes would have been uninhabitable and unnavigable, so did such places represent the edge of civilisation? Was it here where the church had the weakest reach, making the locals a more fearful bunch? What made this area such a draw for Satan? What prompted his frequent appearances to torment the population? He made bets, he stole bells, he claimed souls – yet why *here* more than anywhere else?

The Fens are a place of lawlessness and nature, mists and marshes, willow-the-wisps and wildmen. They're drained and much drier now, yet the feeling of isolation still exists – small pockets of rebellious, free-thinking people, and areas of remote unknown. Is it any wonder that folk like Hereward the Wake made such places their hideout? Or that Samuel Pepys called my home village of Parson Drove a "heathen place" in his famous diary? Fenland people and places have no need for outside influence or interference, and their stories and spirits are there to protect that proud tradition by confounding and confusing outsiders.

Norwich, where I now call home, is the region's largest city – built layer upon layer by the many communities that have settled here over the centuries. From its Anglo Saxon foundations to the Dane Invasion, the Norman Conquest and into the medieval era, its locations, and the connecting cobbled streets and alleys, are intrinsic to the distinctive character of the city to this day. Even in 2021, it's easy to imagine the fighters of Ketts Rebellion hiding in dark night-time doorways, ready to torch buildings. Buildings such as Cow Tower and the ancient city walls remain prominent reminders that history is all around you, even in our modern day. And down below are a multitude of undercrofts and tunnels that criss-cross the entire city, radiating out from the Castle, the Cathedral and other key landmarks. Many of these networks are known, some are rumoured, some may not exist at all – but as you walk through the ancient marketplace of Tombland, or its surrounding streets, I dare you not to feel and wonder what lies beneath your feet.

In the region just north of Norwich, but not quite reaching the coast, lies an area where witches and rituals prevail in tales of yore. Dark, wooded groves and creepy, bare-branched heathlands create pockets of spooky and sometimes oppressive atmosphere – especially as dusk gradually creeps into night. Overgrown church ruins in thickets of woods, and bare trees with nothing but crows sitting in them, watching. There are rumours of druidic sacrificial rituals at such locations – places like The Great Stone of Lyng; places where it feels like you're being watched, and it feels *witchy*.

If you travel the corridor stretching from the coast, through Castle Acre down via Thetford and into deeper Suffolk, you can sense two groups of people: Pilgrims travelling northward to the various abbeys en route, and Iceni warriors heading south. There are sites of battles covering Roman, Saxon and Danes – it's bloodier for sure, but somehow brighter, as if steeped in history rather than superstition. What characters have walked those sandy paths, for what reason, and for what cause were they fighting as they passed through?

As far East as you can go in Britain is the Suffolk coast, a windswept and beautiful though desolate place. The sea has left its mark here, eroding the land, and taking with it entire cities such as in the case of world-worn Dunwich. Sea, storms and smugglers prevail, and the landscape bears their marks. The beaches at Covehithe and Dunwich have a sense of loss hanging over them: bare-bleached tree-trunks laying on the sand; a single gravestone clinging on at the cliff-top, soon to join hundreds of others in the watery grave below. Is it a coincidence that this loss-filled landscape was also the area where Hopkins the Witchfinder tortured and executed the majority of his victims, inflicting loss and trauma en masse on the communities to whom it was home?

Black Shuck appeared during a truly fearsome East Anglian storm, a storm so violent that it was still written about centuries later. Of all the places where myths are formed and legends are born, of all the places in the world to manifest...

HE CHOSE HERE.

COLONEL THOMAS SYDNEY OF RANWORTH WAS A RENOWNED NORFOLK VILLAIN

Famous for his foul temper, being a drunkard and a braggart, handy with his fists and willing to do anything to win, the dreaded colonel resided in **Ranworth Hall**, out in the Norfolk broads. He oversaw village events with an iron will and cruel temperament, and both villagers and farmhands feared and respected his awful character.

Every year Sydney held a hunt, and every year he challenged a fellow huntsman to a race on horseback. Every year, Sydney won. This was through a mixture of his undeniable riding skill, but also because no rival dare beat him for fear of later repercussions.

Until, that is, the race of the **1770 Ranworth hunt**. As per tradition, Sydney challenged a fellow rider, but this time with an extra wager thrown into the bargain.

THE DEVIL COULD TAKE THE LOSER.

The race was hard and close, but as they neared the final stretch it became clear that Sydney would be bested. This would not stand. Sydney drew his pistol and shot his opponent's steed from under him, killing both horse and rider, and sealing Sydney's victory.

Victorious, roaring drunk and unchallenged at that night's ball, Sydney celebrated without shame or remorse. However, he was soon in for a shock: the Devil did indeed claim the loser's soul, but having witnessed the foul play he decided to also take the victor!

Appearing at the door of Ranworth Hall, a tall dark figure crossed the threshold, strode through the feast and snatched Sydney. He carried him back out, threw him across the saddle of his fearsome black mount, and galloped away across the broad. Thomas Sydney was never seen again.

Every New Year's Eve however, furious hooves and the cries of a drunk can be heard deep within the mists that rise mysteriously from the broad without fail.

Tiddy Munn is the king of the Tiddy people, a race of mischevious impish fellows who live in the fens, described by EH Rudkin in 1955 as **"They be tiddy critturs, no more than a span high, wi' arms and legs as thin as thread, but great big feet an' hands, an' heads rollin' aboot on their shoulders."**

They helped fenland crops grow, acted as guides through the marsh, and it was an honour for one to visit your soggy hovel.

Their king Tiddy Munn himself stood three feet high and could control all aspects of the wetlands - from the tides, to the wildlife and fowl, and even the swirling mists. The elements were his to command, and he saved many villages from flooding when heeding the peasants' prayer of:

"TIDDY MUNN, WI' OUT A NAME, THA WATTERS THRUFF!"

When he heard the prayer, he would leap into action with a laugh similar to the call of a peewit - and the waters would recede. Fen folk and Tiddy people lived in harmony.

This all changed when efforts began to drains the fens. Witnessing outsiders destroy his watery kingdom, **Tiddy Munn became enraged**. Soon livestock fell ill, crops failed, and travellers began to go missing in the marshes - all as a result of the Tiddy Munn curse.

The only way to hold a fragile truce was for villagers to regularly fill the dykes and drains with fresh water, whilst chanting a new prayer:

"TIDDY MUNN, WI' OUT A NAME, HERE'S WATER FOR THEE, TAK THE SPELL UNDONE!"

TIDDY MUHN

THE TOADMEN WERE A SECRETIVE GROUP OF FENLAND HORSE WHISPERERS, ABLE TO TAME THE WILDEST STALLIONS WITH EASE.

WAS THEIR POWER MAGICAL, SATANIC OR NATURAL? READ THEIR RITUAL AND DECIDE FOR YOURSELF.

"

I hung the limp toad up to dry
Overnight on a blackthorn tree, like Shecky said,
Then stuffed it in an anthill for a month,
And by the full moon's light pulled out a chain
Of bones, picked clean.
Then came the tricky part.
You carry the skeleton to a running stream
To ride the moonlit water, but you dare not
Take your eyes off it till a certain bone
Rises and floats uphill against the current;
Then grab this bone—a little crotch bone it is,
Shaped like a horse's hoof—and take it home,
Bake it and break it up into a powder:
The power's in the powder. *"*

JOHN REIBETANZ - SAM APPLEBY, HORSEMAN

TOM HICKATHRIFT

THE FENLAND GIANT

HE ALSO:

Could carry an impossible weight of straw.

Defended Ely from an army of 10,000 men, using a 'lusty rawboned miller' as a weapon.

Kicked a huge boulder a distance greater than 2 miles, where it crashed into a church.

TOM HICKATHRIFT is one of the most famous fellas in Fenland folklore. Growing up in the parish of **Marshland St James** deep within the desolate Smeeth between Wisbech and Kings Lynn, Tom was an affable yet lazy young man who stood eight feet tall and was blessed with great strength.

In the most famous of his exploits, written by John Weever in **1631**, we are told about an ogre who lives out in the marsh, making a living through terror, skullduggery and robbery of lonely traders as they trekked their caravans across the Smeeth. On one occasion whilst on an errand pulling a wagon of beer barrels to Kings Lynn, Tom stumbled across such a robbery in progress.

Without hesitation, Tom leapt to the peasants' aid! Tearing the axle and wheel from his wagon, and brandishing them as a crude club and shield, he bravely set about the ogre.

"A TURD IN YOUR TEETH FOR YOUR NEWS, FOR YOU SHALL NOT FIND ME AS ONE OF THEM!"

he yelled as he attacked.

After a fierce battle, Tom battered the ogre to death, and on searching the vile beast's cave, found many a treasure plundered from the fen folk over the years. Tom distributed the wealth back amongst the villagers and was deservedly heralded as the Hero of the Marsh!

But that wasn't all for Tom: with his new-found fame, he went on to lead the most interesting of lives - fighting bandits, slaying giants and dragons, and on one occasion even beating the Devil himself at a game of football.

After adventures all across England and beyond, he eventually returned to the Smeeth of his youth to live out his years and die a peaceful death. He is buried in the graveyard at **Tilney all Saints**, where his grave is still visible and visitable to this day.

Norwich's ancient marketplace, **Tombland**, is rife with history and ghost stories. Whether is it the ghosts of Oliver Cromwell's troops beheaded by chains strung across secret underground tunnels under the **Maids Head Hotel**, or indeed the Grey Maid who haunts the hotel itself; the living statues of Samson and Hercules just next door, or the spirit of fire-and-brimstone preacher **Father Ignatius** who curses passersby on nearby Elm Hill to damnation, or one of many other tales, Tombland - as the centre of medieval Norwich - is a hub of the city's dark tapestry of history.

NO STORY IS MORE PROMINENT, NOR MORE SAD, THAN THE STORY OF THE CROOKED AND ANCIENT AUGUSTINE STEWARD HOUSE.

The crooked and beautiful **Augustine Steward house,** which stands directly opposite the Cathedral's **Erpingham Gate,** is possibly one of the most photographed buildings in all of East Anglia. Built in 1530 for Augustine Steward - famous for being the King's negotiator with Robert Kett during Kett's Rebellion - the house was used for lodgings by the King's troops who were sent to quash the uprising. Amongst the ranks was **Lord Sheffield** who was slain in battle close to the cathedral and now haunts the nearby Adam and Eve pub.

However, it was during the outbreak of the **Black Death in 1576** that the house entered infamy. As plague took hold throughout the city, various properties were condemned and boarded up - *some with victims still inside* - in the hope this would slow the spread of the plague. The Augustine Steward House was identified as ridden with infection, and promptly sealed up. People mourned the loss of the distinguished husband and wife inside.

Once the plague had passed, the house was once more unsealed. It was only then that the citizens realised their terrible mistake. When the house had been boarded up, it was known that a wealthy couple had lived there - but their teenage daught had been completely forgotten about. Trapped and nailed inside, and unable to rais the alarm, her house had slowly become her tomb - but not before she had been forced to resort to cannibalism of her parents' bodies to try and survive.

SHE WAS FOUND ALONGSIDE THEIR SORE-RIDDEN CORPSES, WITH CHUNKS OF THEIR PUTRID FLESH LODGED IN HER THROAT.

She now haunts the narrow **Tombland Alley** to the side of the house - a sorrowful city-centre spirit, neglected and mournful.

PLAGUE HOUSE
OF TOMBLAND

Front and rear alleyway views on Augustine Steward House

Erpingham gate, directly opposite the house.

Ancient Elm Hill, haunted by the ranting Father Ignatus

THE DEVIL

AND THE BELLS

THERE ARE MANY RUMOURS OF THE DEVIL HERE. THEY ARE ALL TRUE.

On the edge of the Eastern Norfolk marshes lies the small village of **Tunstall**. The last civilised settlement before you reach Great Yarmouth on the coast, Tunstall lies at the boundary where fields and farmland meet uninhabited marshland.

In one notable encounter, in **1704**, the church of **St. Peter and St. Paul** caught ablaze, and as the nave burned fiercely, the rector and church warden began a blazing row about who would save - and retain ownership of - the magnificent church bells. However, whilst they were distracted in argument, another potential claimant saw his opportunity. The Devil did not hesitate and seized his chance!

Appearing in the clouds of soot and smoke, the Devil leapt to the top of the tower, snatched the bells, and made his escape. The rector's pleas to God to intervene were ignored.

As the villagers fruitlessly chased after him across nearby fields and woods, the Devil jumped one final, massive leap - before plummeting through the earth and back down to the underworld with his bounty. The impact from his leap created a hollow, which soon became a pond. To this day, that pond is known locally as **the Hellhole**, and the clump of trees in which it is situated is known as **Hellcarr**.

IT IS SAID THAT THE POND STILL BUBBLES CONSTANTLY TO THIS DAY, AS THE DEVIL AND THE BELLS CONTINUE TO SINK INTO HELLHOLE'S FATHOMLESS DEPTHS, EVEN CENTURIES LATER.

TUNSTALL

CHURCH

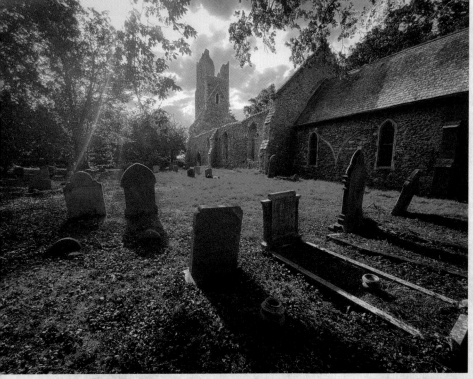

IN 1127 - IN GRIMESHAW WOODS, ON THE OUTSKIRTS OF PETERBOROUGH - A TERRIBLE AND FEARSOME NOISE WAS HEARD.

Strangely coinciding with the appointment of **Henry d'Angely** - a corrupt and incompetent abbott at the Benedictine monastery at Peterborough - the forests between Peterborough and Stamford rang with blasted horns, and the stampeding of hooves. It continued every night for nine weeks, and townsfolk and villagers cowered in fear, convinced it was a portent of doom.

Its story was described in detail by a monk from the abbey who wrote in the Peterborough Chronicle that same year:

"1127 Let it not be thought remarkable, the truth of what we say, because it was fully known over all the land, that immediately after Henry came there, then soon afterwards many men saw and heard many huntsmen hunting.

"THE HUNTSMEN WERE BLACK AND HUGE AND LOATHSOME, AND THEIR HOUNDS ALL BLACK AND WIDE-EYED AND LOATHSOME, AND THEY RODE ON BLACK HORSES AND ON BLACK BILLY-GOATS.

"This was seen in the very deer-park of the town of Peterborough, and in all the woods there were from that same town to Stamford; and the monks heard the horns blow that they blew in the night. Honest men who kept watch in the night said that it seemed to them there might well have been about twenty or thirty horn-blowers. This was seen and heard from when he came there, all that Lenten-tide right up to Easter. This was his entrance: of his exit we cannot yet say. May God provide!"

Other reliable sources also documented this terrifying event and it has gone down in history as one of the first known Wild Hunts, which have now passed into legend throughout Europe. It is sometimes considered that either **Hereward the Wake** or **Saint Guthlac** may have summoned the hunt, but no-one knows the truth of why these pitch-black barbarians appeared, or why they left. Was it a judgement on Henry that has now passed, or do they still lurk out there in Grimeshaw Woods waiting for the next chance to sound their horns and charge once more?

WILD HUNT

Out in the furthest reaches of North Norfolk, down a lonely track to nowhere, and nestled within an ancient overgrown wood, lie possibly the most evocative and atmospheric ruins in the entire region.

Built in the **15th Century**, St. Mary's Church in **East Somerton** was the site of a witch's trial. Found guilty and sentenced to death, she was *buried alive*.

BUT HER VENGEFUL SPIRIT REFUSED TO SLEEP.

From her wooden leg, her spirit caused a great tree to grow, and - slowly, but very definitely surely - it eventually reached the church roof. It carried on growing, up and finally through the roof, which then came crashing down on the worshipping monks who had acted as the judge, jury and executioner of the witch. The falling roof served as the witch's revenge, killing the monks below and driving the church to ruin in the 17th Century.

The tree remains to this day - a monument to revenge. It is told that if you circle it thrice, the witch will leap from her grave to wreak vengeance once more.

You may also catch a glimpse of the ghostly monks in the undergrowth, and it is said by some that the murder of crows that caw high in the tree-tops of this dark and sinister glade are their spirits, warning explorers to leave their place of worship to the wilds.

THANK YOU.

I SINCERELY HOPE YOU HAVE ENJOYED THIS TRIP THROUGH SOME OF MY FAVOURITE EAST ANGLIAN TALES AS MUCH I ENJOYED RESEARCHING, VISITING, DRAWING AND WRITING ABOUT THEM.

THE STORIES IN THIS BOOK BARELY SCRATCH THE SURFACE. THERE ARE MANY, MANY MORE EXTRAORDINARY TALES TO BE TOLD AND DISCOVERED - WHEREVER YOU MAY CALL HOME. HOPEFULLY THESE TALES HAVE SPARKED SOME INTEREST IN YOU TO UNCOVER MORE FOR YOURSELF, OR DIVE DEEPER INTO THE STORIES I HAVE SHARED HERE.

I TRULY BELIEVE IT'S MORE IMPORTANT THAN EVER TO CONNECT WITH THE PEOPLE AND PLACES CLOSE TO US, AND THAT THROUGH THESE CONNECTIONS WE LEARN MORE ABOUT THE WORLD AND OUR PLACE IN IT. THESE STORIES MAY COME FROM A SIMPLER AND LESS CYNICAL TIME, BUT PERHAPS THAT'S WHAT THE WORLD NEEDS RIGHT NOW.

I WISH YOU ALL THE LUCK AND GOOD HEALTH OUT THERE. EXPLORE MORE, READ MORE, CONNECT MORE AND CREATE MORE. FOLLOW THAT FOOTPATH ACROSS THAT FIELD - WHO KNOWS WHAT YOU MIGHT FIND?

THANKS AGAIN, YOUR SUPPORT AND INTEREST IS GREATLY APPRECIATED.

CHRIS SPALTON.
~NORWICH, APRIL 2021